From My Heart

A Collection of Poems

By Siyoda Jayawardene

Illustrated by Roger Grose

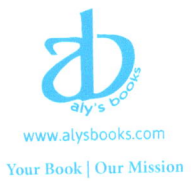

www.alysbooks.com
Your Book | Our Mission

I dedicate my book to my beloved parents and also my teachers.

Siyoda

From My Heart
A Collection of Poems

Copyright © Siyoda Jayawardene
Illustration copyright © Roger Grose

First Edition 2014
Published by Aly's Books

www.alysbooks.com
Your Book | Our Mission

Edited by Irrefutable Proof
www.irrefutable-proof.com

Designed by Nitty Gritty Graphics

All rights reserved. No part of this book may be reproduced or transmitted in any form or by any means, electronic, mechanical, photocopying or otherwise without the prior permission of the publisher.

ISBN: 978-0-9941767-3-8

Foreword

I knew Siyoda as a gifted child skillful in many facets of the arts – singing, acting and dancing. Recently she achieved celebrity status among the Sri Lankan community in Melbourne as the presenter of the children's program of the Sri Lanka Morning Show on Channel 31. The list of this little girl's capabilities does not end there. Her latest, this book of poems, adds a shining star to her already bright string of achievements.

Siyoda would write her own verses on birthday cards to her friends from a very young age. The parents of her friends admired and talked about her sophisticated yet beautiful writing. She started to pen verses about her surroundings while travelling in the back seat of the family car, expressing her feelings about what she saw in a poetic way. Her teachers noticed the emerging writing skill in this little girl as early as the second grade.

Encouraged by parents of her friends and her teachers, Siyoda's parents Dhammika and Ruwan decided to publish a collection of the poems she has written so far. This book has been the final outcome.

It seems that the environment Siyoda lives in has given her a lot of food for thought. Her poems showcase her creativity and appreciation of the little world surrounding her; nature, family and animals. This book testifies to that.

The illustrations, done by Roger Grose, Willmott Park Primary School Arts Teacher, have added another dimension to this book and invite the reader to immerse themselves in the poetry.

Having a desire to excel, self-motivation, energy and skills nourished with further learning, Siyoda will be able to achieve her dreams. I am sure there will be more to come. I wish her good luck!

Vijaya Karunasena
Former Producer, Sinhala Program, SBS Radio

Ballerina

She swirls and twirls
She's prettier than pearls!
That's the way she is…
She points and dances,
She's flexible and prances
It would be great if she was your sis…
She is really fit
Not fat a bit
And has a big ballet kit.

She dances so nice
Don't forget she's wise
Because she's a BALLERINA!!!

Dancing

We can jig
Wearing a wig
We dance
Or even prance!
So come along and join the fun
There's something to do for everyone!

Tap to the left (tap tap)
Clap to the right (clap clap)
Do it until the middle of night
Tap to the right
Clap to the left
Do it until you're out of breath.

Froggy Day

"It's Froggy day,
 So come out and play,
 It's fun for everyone."

"But frogs are slimy,
 Sticky and so icky.
 It's not fun for everyone."

"I love the sliminess,
 Stickiness and ickiness,
 So come and have a taste."

"I'm sure you like it,
 But if I try it,
 It'll certainly be,
 Lots of waste!"

Frogs

Gruesome feet that
are really not sweet
Bulging eyes
With croaky cries
That's the little green frog.
Blue, yellow, black and green
Camouflaged, cannot be seen
Dry little croaks fill the night
Even when there is a single light.
Frogs are all amphibians
I know one that's named Big Lion.

Trees

Trees are the peacefulest
Things I know
They do no harm they
Just grow and grow.

Trees, trees, trees
Everybody knows
They may grow high
They may grow low.

Trees are the first to
Touch sunlight
They are the last to
See moonlight.

Trees, trees, trees
Such wonderful things
They don't harm
Any human beings!

Season

Summer's come
Spring's past
The seasons fly
By really fast

Spring

Spring is pure as a ring
It makes you want to swing
Spring is bright
Just like a light
It's a pleasant thing
The flowers bloom
Excites the room
Animals come out
And run about
It's time to give my puppy a groom

Flower Magic

Flower garden is
Lovely to see
Orange, peach flowers packed with buzzing bees
Wow! Go the children who see such entertainment
Endless hearts filled with joy and amazement
Rabbits butterflies and pretty birds
Magical and mystical jolly words
Animals and humans all enjoy
Getting together like little toys
In flower garden it's so fun
Children and adults rate it number ONE!

Insect Garden!

Insects are free to move around
Not one of them are the
Same, each insect is unique or
Exquisite
Catching prey
Thinking of a place to be safe.

Green gruesome eyes watch every single move
Alert at all times.
Red, green, brown and blue, there are many types
Different insects
Every day they are
Not fully safe or harmed.

Summer

So hot that I barely can't move
Umbrellas prevent me from sunburn
Melting ice-cream
Must go to the pool
Everyone's sweaty
Re-hydrating with water

A summer's touch

The blazing sun looks down at me
A light I cannot deny
The grass has gone chocolate brown
And has no more tears to cry.

Tiny drops of sticky sweat
Pour down my oily face
I get sunburn, I don't wanna learn
Gee… this is disgrace.

Refreshing cool icy poles
Relax me down, down, down
It makes me really happy
As a jolly good old clown.

Tiny filthy stinky ants
Invade our households foods
Like cookies, lollies, and some meat
Which are all our goods.

Summer, summer, summer
It is the best season yet
That's one comment I really do bet.

Stormy Night

On stormy nights
There are no lights
You can't find the way!
Thunder roars, lightning strikes
It makes you frightened today.
You're all alone
You miss your home
And wish that you should've stayed.
The wind blows
The twigs flow
It's to the rhythm of the rain.
If you get struck by lightning
You know…
It's really such a pain!

Rain

Round balls wet the ground
Always they are transparent
In the sky they are waiting to drop down
Naughty children play in the rain.

Pitter-patter on the ground
I can hear the raindrop sound.
It's lighter than an ink blue pen
Come on rain, do it again.

Raindrops, raindrops they are cold
Raindrops, raindrops never get old.

Windy Days

On a windy day like this,
You will begin to miss,
The wonderful times on the beach,
When you splish, splosh, splash with your feet.

On a windy day like this,
You will never ever miss,
Flying a kite around in the sky,
It might even go up so high…

On windy days it's such a blast!
How the wind swoops really fast!

The Beach

Suddenly SPLASH!
I hear the waves crash,
Along the sandy shore.
Seagulls squawk,
People talk,
There are children galore!
The golden sand,
Wriggles through my feet,
It reminds me of worms,
That I hate to eat!

The golden sun beams at me,
It fills my heart with happiness and glee!
Come to the beach,
It's so, so fun,
There's something to do for everyone!

The Weird Dog

There once was a dog
Who ate a log?
He couldn't talk
Nor could he walk
He then turned into a frog

Friends

Friends are the people you can
Rely on
If you're in danger they'll help you
Escape
New or old friend
Depend on you like you depend on them
Sri Lankan or Australian we're all friends…

Anzac Day

Bang! Goes the gun
There is not time to run
Crackle, sizzle pop!
Sad families will sob
The air is filled with smoke
Someone could choke.

There are painful moans
And terrible groans
Oh! The sound
It's so loud!
The soldiers scream
It's so not a dream.

The soldiers are fighting
It's fast as lighting
To see who will win.

But when Gallipoli won
They put their grin on
And celebrated on that day
Shouting 'Hip Hip Hooray!'

How could they see?
It was black as could be
Only the stars to light the way
See how lucky we are today.
All the soldiers sacrificed their lives
It was not so easy like giving high fives
All the soldiers did it for us
They didn't even ride a bus.

So that's how all our troops fought
They are way braver than I thought!

Mice

They scamper across your house
At night
They make no sound
But give you a fright!
They're very small
Compared to a ball
But they run in the blink
Of an eye.
Before you can even
Say "Bye!"
Mice have little
Razor sharp teeth
But we never ever even
Hear them breathe
Mice mice mice
Such horrid guests
They're really awful tiny pests!

Panic

The sirens wailed like old tom cats,
The big black wheels screeched like bats,
People yelled and screamed for their lives,
There was certainly no time to give high fives.
The air smelt of dull, grey smoke,
People were going to hospital, that's no joke!
It's a fight against time,
I heard a police alarm chime.
It's an emergency so they go there quick,
The fire-brigade drives off in a click,
This situation is so not fun,
You would never ever want to be in one.

The Cat

I know a skinny cat
Who ate and became fat
One day my brother said
"Hey, the CAT is dead!"
And I found him on my
mum's sunhat.

Parents

Papa, Mama, Mum or Dad
All our parents are people we can't describe
Respecting us like we do to them
Everyone loves their parents
Normal or extraordinary
They do all the things for us
Sometimes strict.

The Memory of Lanka

The icy-blue water looks at me
A free young girl now I see
Dancing swiftly like a palm
Always, always really calm.

A girl sings a song
And says come along
Join the fun with me
Come, come, come…
You'll rate it number one
So sing this song with me.

The streams in Lanka
Gently pour
Wow! Look at the beauty
You can't possibly ask for more.

Green tea leaves catch drops of dew
All of them catch at least a few
Scenting the air a nourishing smell
Makes me want to stay and dwell.

Little dogs walking down the street
Happy to eat, meet and greet
Please can I have a little home?
Even if it's the size of a gnome.

Sri Lanka, Sri Lanka
So gorgeous too
I always, always think of you!

My Life Stage

When I was ONE I had just begun
When I was TWO I liked the colour blue
When I was THREE I was happy as could be
When I was FOUR I hit the floor
When I was FIVE I learnt to dive
When I was SIX I loved Weetbix
When I was SEVEN it felt like heaven
When I was EIGHT oh, life was great
When I was NINE I was doing fine
Now I am TEN so
I'll start again!

Acknowledgements

I would like to thank my parents for their unconditional support and guidance on this project.

I was inspired to write poems by my parents. I loved singing and many elements of poetry go in to songs; like rhythm and rhyme. I have been gifted with so many poetry books in the last couple of years by my mum and dad. I also read many Dr. Seuss books when I was young. They also contain poetry.

During my free time, I like to draw, play with my friends, sing and dance. I am also currently in speech and drama competitions. I love music, dancing, speech and drama, writing and art.

I chose to help the charity Sole because most children in rural areas of Sri Lanka do not have proper school shoes, and they wear thongs to school or go to school with bare feet. I realised there is a big value in helping them as we have more benefits and facilities in our schools in Victoria. I feel that every child in the world should have equal benefits as we are all the same. Most money raised through my book will go to Sole's charity work. Sole has started their charity work from Galle District Batuwangala School. All the shoes will be manufactured through a special needs unit. It is a two way job helping the community in Sri Lanka.

Special thanks to my art teacher Mr Roger Grose for all his hard work creating these astounding illustrations. Also I would like to thank Mr Vijaya Karunasena for writing the foreword of my very first book. A big thanks goes to Mrs. Aly Walsh for designing and publishing my book.

Last but not least I would like to thank my teachers Miss Luci Scamarcio, Miss Michelle Tedeschi and Mrs Sashini Alexander for guiding me along the way.

www.ingramcontent.com/pod-product-compliance
Lightning Source LLC
Chambersburg PA
CBHW042052290426
44110CB00001B/39